SEASONS OF THE YEAR

Summer

by Rebecca Pettiford

BELLWETHER MEDIA • MINNEAPOLIS, MN

Note to Librarians, Teachers, and Parents:

Blastoff! Readers are carefully developed by literacy experts and combine standards-based content with developmentally appropriate text.

Level 1 provides the most support through repetition of high-frequency words, light text, predictable sentence patterns, and strong visual support.

Level 2 offers early readers a bit more challenge through varied simple sentences, increased text load, and less repetition of high-frequency words.

Level 3 advances early-fluent readers toward fluency through increased text and concept load, less reliance on visuals, longer sentences, and more literary language.

Level 4 builds reading stamina by providing more text per page, increased use of punctuation, greater variation in sentence patterns, and increasingly challenging vocabulary.

Level 5 encourages children to move from "learning to read" to "reading to learn" by providing even more text, varied writing styles, and less familiar topics.

Whichever book is right for your reader, Blastoff! Readers are the perfect books to build confidence and encourage a love of reading that will last a lifetime!

This edition first published in 2018 by Bellwether Media, Inc.

No part of this publication may be reproduced in whole or in part without written permission of the publisher. For information regarding permission, write to Bellwether Media, Inc., Attention: Permissions Department, 5357 Penn Avenue South, Minneapolis, MN 55419.

Library of Congress Cataloging-in-Publication Data

Names: Pettiford, Rebecca, author.
Title: Summer / by Rebecca Pettiford.
Description: Minneapolis, MN : Bellwether Media, 2018. | Series: Blastoff!
    Readers: Seasons of the Year | Includes bibliographical references and
    index. | Audience: K-3.
Identifiers: LCCN 2017029525 | ISBN 9781626177628 (hardcover : alk. paper)
    | ISBN 9781681034676 (ebook) | ISBN 9781618913036 (pbk. : alk. paper)
Subjects: LCSH: Summer–Juvenile literature.
Classification: LCC QB637.6 .P48 2018 | DDC 508.2–dc23
LC record available at https://lccn.loc.gov/2017029525

Editor: Christina Leaf   Designer: Josh Brink

Printed in the United States of America, North Mankato, MN.

Table of Contents

fireflies

Chirp! Crickets sing as fireflies **twinkle**. Lightning flashes across the distant sky.

The warm air is sticky.
It smells like cut grass.
This is summer!

When Is Summer?

Summer starts after spring ends. In the **Northern Hemisphere**, summer begins in June.

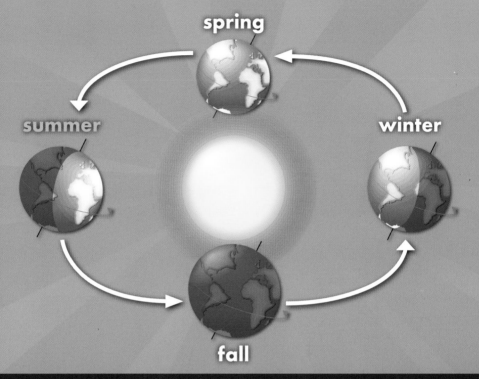

Earth's Position in Summer

spring

summer

winter

fall

Seasons change with the amount of sunlight reaching Earth. The Northern Hemisphere is tilted toward the sun in summer, so it receives more sunlight.

The other summer months are July and August.

Summer Weather

In summer, Earth **tilts** toward the sun. This makes the days long and hot.

Warm summer air often holds a lot of water. This **humidity** brings rain and thunderstorms.

Summer brings **hurricanes**. These powerful storms form over warm ocean water.

Hurricane season begins June 1

Hurricane Risk in Summer

highest   high   moderate

Their strong, swirling winds can destroy buildings and trees.

Plants and Animals in Summer

With so much sunlight in summer, plants grow quickly. Trees have full green leaves.

Flowers bloom in gardens and **wildflowers** spring up in grassy fields.

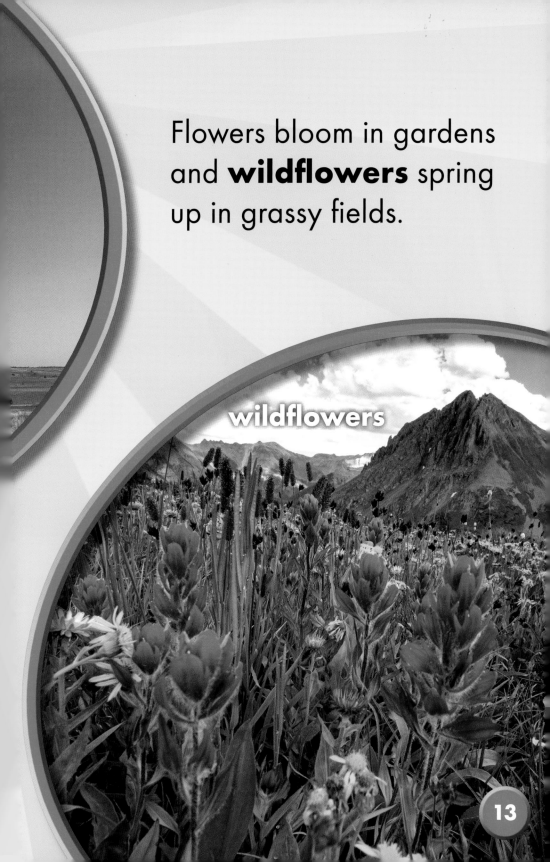

wildflowers

harvesting wheat

Farmers **harvest** summer corn and hay from fields.

Berries and other fruits ripen. Gardens overflow with fresh vegetables.

strawberries

Summer is the best time for animals to raise their young. Food is easy to find.

mother deer and fawn

mountain lion

Predators hunt baby animals.
But with many babies around,
everyone has a good chance
to survive.

Animals escape the heat.
Some **shed** thick fur coats.

mountain goat
shedding fur

bald eagle

Birds splash in streams. Fish find cooler waters. **Reptiles** rest under rocks or in **burrows**.

In summer, people cool off
at the beach or pool.

They eat and drink frosty treats. They enjoy every last drop of summer!

Glossary

burrows—holes or tunnels that some animals dig for homes

harvest—to gather or pick crops

humidity—the amount of water in the air

hurricanes—large, powerful storms with swirling winds that form over warm ocean waters

Northern Hemisphere—the half of the globe that lies north of the equator; the equator is an imaginary line around Earth.

predators—animals that hunt other animals for food

reptiles—cold-blooded animals that have backbones and lay eggs

shed—to lose fur or hair

tilts—slants or tips

twinkle—to shine with bright points of light

wildflowers—flowers that grow without being planted by people

To Learn More

AT THE LIBRARY
Farndon, John. *Weather.* New York, N.Y.: DK Publishing, 2017.

Owen, Ruth. *How Do You Know It's Summer?* New York, N.Y.: Bearport Publishing, 2012.

Rice, William. *The Seasons.* Huntington Beach, Calif.: Teacher Created Materials, 2015.

ON THE WEB
Learning more about summer is as easy as 1, 2, 3.

1. Go to www.factsurfer.com.

2. Enter "summer" into the search box.

3. Click the "summer" button and you will see a list of related web sites.

With factsurfer.com, finding more information is just a click away.

Index